To Laura

THE BIGGEST BURP EVER

Funny Poems for Kids

Have a gas!

Kenn Nesbitt

FEB 2015

Illustrations by
Rafael Domingos

Published by
Purple Room Publishing
1314 S Grand Blvd #2-321
Spokane, Washington 99202

Fax: 815-642-8206

www.poetry4kids.com

For Zoe

Contents

The Biggest Burp Ever

The record, so far, for the world's biggest burp
is held by Belinda Melinda McNurp.
It wasn't on purpose. She wasn't to blame.
Her tummy just rumbled, and out the burp came.

Belinda then instantly saw her mistake.
The ground began trembling and starting to shake.
That rumble was suddenly more of a roar.
It busted the windows and knocked down the door.

Her mother and father both covered their ears.
Her brother and sister were nearly in tears.
Her puppy looked panicked and yipped as he fled.
Her kitten just cowered and covered his head.

The cars on the street began skidding and stopping.
The shoppers in shops started dropping their shopping.
The squirrels all burrowed. The birds flew away.
The sun disappeared for the rest of the day

as clouds began thundering all around town.
The trees toppled over. The buildings fell down.
Tornadoes and hurricanes blew through the sky.
The rivers flowed backward. The oceans ran dry.

Volcanoes erupted from Perth to Peru.
The Grand Canyon widened. Mount Everest grew.
The earth started spinning a different direction.
And, worst of all, I lost my iPhone connection.

Belinda was pretty embarrassed alright,
but she was well-mannered, and very polite.
And that's why she knew it would all be okay
when she said, "Excuse me," and went on her way.

Xbox, Xbox

Xbox, Xbox,
you're the one for me.
I also love my 3DS
and my Nintendo Wii.

GameCube, GameBoy,
Apple iPod Touch.
I never thought that I would ever
be in love this much.

Pac-Man, Sonic,
Mario, and Link.
Your names are etched inside my mind
in everlasting ink.

Run, jump, flip, hang,
double-jump, and climb.
That's all I want to do
with every second of my time.

This is true love.
Yes, it's plain to see.
Xbox, Xbox,
will you marry me?

My Mother Said to Do My Chores

My mother said to do my chores,
to dust the shelves and mop the floors,
and wipe the walls and wind the clocks,
and scoop the kitty's litter box,
and walk the dog and feed the fishes,
and wash and dry the dirty dishes,
and clean my room and take a bath,
and read a book and do my math,
and pick up all my Lego blocks,
and put away my shoes and socks,
and hang my shirts and fold my pants,
and water all the potted plants,
and organize my toys and games,
and straighten up the picture frames,
and polish all the silverware,
and brush my teeth and comb my hair,
and rake the leaves and mow the lawn,
and on and on and on and on.

She said I'll get to have some fun
as soon as all my chores are done.

With all the chores I have to do
until my mother says I'm through,
like study for an hour or two,
and peel potatoes and stir the stew,
and fix a vase with crazy glue,
and practice tuba till I'm blue,
and wash the dog with pet shampoo,
and sweep the chimney and the flue,
and scrub the tub and toilet too,
and pick up piles of puppy poo...

It looks like I'll be ninety three
before I get to watch TV.

My Dog Lives on the Sofa

My dog lives on the sofa.
That's where he wants to be.
He likes to sit there night and day
and watch what's on TV.
He surfs the channels constantly
by chewing the remote,
then watches what he wants to watch;
I never get a vote.

He's fond of films with animals.
He takes in nature shows.
Whenever cat cartoons come on
he always watches those.
He loves the pet commercials too,
and anything with food.
Whenever there's a tennis match
he nearly comes unglued.
I got him from the dog pound.
He didn't cost a cent.
I asked them for a "watch dog,"
but this isn't what I meant.

I Didn't Go Camping

I didn't go camping.
I didn't go hiking.
I didn't go fishing.
I didn't go biking.

I didn't go play
on the slides at the park.
I didn't watch shooting stars
way after dark.

I didn't play baseball
or soccer outside.
I didn't go on an
amusement park ride.

I didn't throw Frisbees.
I didn't fly kites,
or have any travels,
or see any sights.

I didn't watch movies
with blockbuster crowds,
or lay on the front lawn
and look at the clouds.

I didn't go swimming
at pools or beaches,
or visit an orchard
and pick a few peaches.

I didn't become
a guitarist or drummer,
but, boy, I played plenty
of Minecraft this summer.

Cookies for Santa

I baked a dozen cookies
and I put them on a plate,
and I set them out for Santa Claus,
except for one I ate.

That cookie was amazing
and I couldn't quite resist...
so I ate another one
that I was sure would not be missed.

I knew it wouldn't matter
if I only ate one more.
Then I gobbled up another one.
Why not? That's only four.

I accidentally dropped
another couple on the ground.
I knew Santa wouldn't want them
so I swiftly scarfed them down.

Another couple disappeared.
I may have eaten those,
though I couldn't say for certain,
but I guess that's how it goes.

I figured four was likely more
than Santa Claus would need,
so I polished off another few
with unexpected speed.

Before I knew what happened
all the damage had been done,
and I realized I'd accidentally
eaten every one.

I guess it's best, since Santa
sort of needs to watch his weight.
When he visits us this Christmas
I sure hope he likes the plate.

Wayne the Stegosaurus

Meet the stegosaurus, Wayne.
He doesn't have the biggest brain.
He's long and heavy, wide and tall,
but has a brain that's extra small.

He's not the brightest dinosaur.
He thinks that one plus one is four.
He can't remember up from down.
He thinks the sky is chocolate brown.

He wears his bow tie on his tail
and likes to eat the daily mail.
When playing hide-and-seek he tries
to hide by covering his eyes.

He thinks that black is really white.
He's sure the sun comes out at night.
He thinks that water grows on trees
and when it's hot he starts to freeze.

He's happy when he's feeling ill.
He likes to dance by standing still.
And when it's time to go to bed,
he puts bananas on his head.

He thinks his name is Bob, not Wayne,
but that's what happens when your brain
(although you're big and brave and spiny)
is very, very, very tiny.

Captain Talkalot

They call me Captain Talkalot.
I really don't know why.
I only talk when I'm awake.
I'm such a quiet guy.

It's true I talk from sunrise
till the moment I'm in bed,
then spend the evening dreaming
of the things I should have said.

But, really, I don't talk too much.
I just say what I think,
which could be while I'm chewing food,
or guzzling a drink.

I'm sure I sometimes raise my voice,
and now and then I yell.
But that's to be expected
when you've got a tale to tell.

I'd never interrupt someone
if they were speaking first,
unless, of course, I had to,
or I felt like I would burst.

I'm simply not that talkative.
I'll show you all the ways
and tell you all the reasons
though it could take several days.

And when I'm done explaining,
then perhaps you'll tell me why
they call me Captain Talkalot.
I'm such a quiet guy.

My Puppy Likes the Water

My puppy likes the water.
My puppy likes to swim.
I've never seen a puppy
who swims as much as him.

He swims not on the surface,
but only underneath.
And maybe I should warn you,
he has very scary teeth.

Whenever people see him
they're frightened of his grin.
Or maybe it's his lack of fur.
Or maybe it's his fin.

If you should buy a puppy,
just get the kind that barks.
Don't be like me. I bought mine
at a store that just sells sharks.

My Dog Ate My Homework

My dog ate my homework.
That mischievous pup
got hold of my homework
and gobbled it up.

My dog ate my homework.
It's gonna be late.
I guess that the teacher
will just have to wait.

My dog ate my homework.
He swallowed it whole.
I shouldn't have mixed it
with food in his bowl.

The Seefood Diet

I've started on a seefood diet.
I highly recommend you try it.
You eat whatever food you see;
a grape, a crepe, a pear, a pea,
a candy cane, some bubble gum,
a piece of pie, a peach, a plum,

banana pancakes, chicken legs,
a dozen donuts, deviled eggs,
spaghetti noodles, sirloin steaks,
vanilla ice cream, birthday cakes,
a hundred pizzas, chocolate mousse,
and gallon jugs of apple juice.

The seefood diet. Just can't beat it.
Whenever you see food, you eat it.
I'm pretty sure you won't lose weight,
But, what the heck? The food is great!

My Mouse Is Misbehaving

My mouse is misbehaving
and my keyboard's on the fritz.
The computer's not computing,
but is dropping bytes and bits.

The hard drive's click-click-clicking
and the printer's spitting ink.
The CD's started stuttering.
The screen is on the blink.

The memory is failing.
Things are grinding to a halt.
And, even worse, I realize
it's probably my fault.

I thought it would be funny.
It was really just a joke.
I never thought the whole computer
might go up in smoke.

I guess I learned my lesson:
When it comes to your PCs,
it's best if you don't ever try
to feed the mouse some cheese.

I'm Not Picky

I'm not picky.
I'm not rude.
Why, I'll eat any
kind of food,
except for foods
called "beets" or "greens"
or "beef" or "beans"
or "tangerines."

I won't eat foods
called "fish fillets"
or "pies" or "fries"
or "mayonnaise"
or "grapes" or "crepes"
or "chicken wings"
or "clams" or "hams"
or "onion rings."

Or anything
called "baked" or "stewed"
or "boiled" or "broiled"
or "barbecued"
or "dried" or "fried"
or "smoked" or "steamed"
or "roasted," "toasted,"
"mashed" or "creamed."

No, I'm not picky.
I'm not rude.
Why, I'll eat any
kind of food,
and ask for more
and then say, "Please,"
as long as it's called
"mac and cheese."

Waiter, There's a Dog in My Soup

There's a doggy in my soup dish.
There's a canine in my cup.
The waiter brought a bowl out
and I found this grubby pup.

His fur is simply sopping.
He's wet from head to toes.
He's got some peas upon his paws
and noodles on his nose.

He doesn't look too happy.
His eyes are filled with tears.
Or maybe that's just chicken soup
that's dripping from his ears.

I'm sure I asked for noodles.
I got this dog instead.
I wonder how this happened.
Was it something that I said?

I guess I must have mumbled.
I'm such a nincompoop!
It seems the waiter heard me ask for
Chicken Poodle Soup.

A Valentine for Mom

I bought a box of chocolates
for my mother's valentine;
a giant, heart-shaped package
with a flowery design.

They had them at the market
and I got the biggest one.
I nearly couldn't pick it up.
It must have weighed a ton.

I had to use a shopping cart
to haul it from the store.
At home I almost couldn't
even fit it through the door.

I gave it to my mother
and you should have seen her eyes!
I clearly had impressed her
with my chocolate box's size.

That carton was gargantuan—
the largest I could find—
but not because I'm generous
and not because I'm kind.

I didn't buy the biggest one
to show how much I care.
I bought it just to guarantee
my mom would have to share.

A Sheep Is Asleep on My Sofa

A sheep is asleep on my sofa.
A sheep is asleep on my floor.
A sheep is asleep in the closet,
and seems to be starting to snore.

A sheep is asleep on my dresser.
A sheep is asleep on my bed.
I found when I woke up this morning,
a sheep was asleep on my head.

A few can be found in the corner.
They're soundly asleep in a heap.
There isn't a space in my bedroom
that isn't all covered in sheep.

With so many sheep in my bedroom,
I'm thinking I wasn't too bright,
and maybe I shouldn't have asked for
a sheepover party last night.

I Love to Do the Laundry

I love to do the laundry.
I mean it. I don't mind
because I get to keep
whatever money I might find.

I know it sounds ridiculous.
I'm sure it must seem strange.
But every time I wash the clothes
I find some pocket change.

I found a dollar yesterday.
Today I found a ten.
I'm certain that tomorrow
I'll find money once again.

You see, I have a strategy.
(I guess that's what you call it.)
And sometimes I just *accidentally*
wash my father's wallet.

Betty Met a Yeti

Betty met a yeti
in the mountains of Tibet.
She cooked him some spaghetti
and she baked him a baguette.
And when the food was ready
and the dishes all were set,
the yeti swallowed Betty
and said, "Mmmm, the best one yet."

So that's the end of Betty,
but you needn't be upset
unless you meet a yeti
in the mountains of Tibet.
Then just stay calm and steady.
Don't be nervous. Never fret.
And *don't* cook him spaghetti
or, who knows what you might get?

I Bought a New Banana Suit

I bought a new banana suit
and new banana shoes.
I stickered up my body with
banana-shaped tattoos.

I also bought banana socks,
a big banana hat,
banana scarf and jewelry,
banana this and that.

Around my face I wrapped
a yellow handkerchief/bandana,
then walked into the market
like an over-sized banana.

I filled a cart with every last
banana in the store,
and when I'd gotten all of them
I headed for the door.

The managers all stopped and stared.
They nearly flipped their lids.
But I just smiled and said to them,
"I'm rescuing my kids."

Mr. Obvious

Hello, I'm Mr. Obvious.
I point out things you know.
I'll tell you that the water's wet.
I'll say that plants can grow.

I might remark that night is dark.
I'll add that grass is green.
And I'll repeat that sugar's sweet
and washing makes you clean.

I'll let you know that snails are slow,
and one plus one is two,
and then declare that squares are square
and state the sky is blue.

You see, I'm kind, so I don't mind
explaining simple things.
And when I do this just for you
I love the joy it brings.

So take a chair and let me share,
and when my lecture ends,
I hope you'll try to tell me why
I don't have any friends.

My Dog Fred

I have a dog.
His name is Fred.
He won't play fetch.
He won't play dead.

He won't shake hands
or sit or stay
or bark or beg
or run and play.

He won't roll over,
jump or crawl.
In fact, he won't
do tricks at all.

When people ask
I tell them that's
because my dog
was raised by cats.

The All-Bean Diet

Beans for breakfast.
Beans for lunch.
Beans for dinner.
Beans for brunch.
Beans for snacks
and all desserts.
Beans until your
stomach hurts.

This is called
the "All-Bean Diet."
Man, it's fun!
You have to try it!
True, it gives you
painful gas...
Still, it sure does
clear the class!

I Eat Spaghetti with a Spoon

I eat spaghetti with a spoon.
For soup I use a fork.
I drink my soda from a bottle
stopped up with a cork.

I have a pair of chopsticks
that I use for cutting cheese,
a spatula for salads,
and a knife for eating peas.

I drink my pizza from a cup,
eat ice cream with a stick,
and when I want a glass of milk
my strainer does the trick.

I slurp salami through a straw.
I don't get too much in.
But that's the way I always stay
so fabulously thin.

While at the Sofa Factory

While at the sofa factory
I nearly broke my spleen
when I accidentally fell in
an upholstery machine.

I almost died that fateful day
but I survived somehow.
And I'm looking even better, too,
since I'm "recovered" now.

My Kitty Likes My Goldfish

My kitty likes my goldfish.
My kitty likes my mice.
My kitty likes my parakeets.
She thinks they're all so nice.

The way she mews so sweetly,
the way she sits and stares,
I'd have to say it's obvious
how much my kitty cares.

She doubtlessly adores them
and thinks so highly of them.
She treats them so attentively
it's clear that she must love them.

But, tragically, they disappeared
the other afternoon.
My kitty seems so lonely now.
I hope they come back soon.

Floyd the Coin Collector

I'm Floyd, the coin collector.
It's coins that I collect.
I'm really not too finicky
with which ones I select.

I like collecting pennies;
they're all I get sometimes.
But often I get nickels, too,
and frequently it's dimes.

I'll gladly keep a dollar coin,
a quarter, or a pound.
I'd even save a rupee
or a ruble that I found.

A euro here, a guilder there,
a peso or a franc;
I'll happily collect them all
and put them in the bank.

My hobby is a simple one;
it's not the least bit strange.
And all you have to do to help
is give me all your change.

My Puppy Makes Pizza

My puppy makes pizza.
He bakes every day
In chef hat and apron
he's quite the gourmet.

He'll roll out some dough
and he'll give it a toss,
then spread on a generous
topping of sauce.
He'll heap it with cheeses
and mountains of meat,
but, still, it's not something
you'd probably eat.
For though he makes pizza
with obvious flair,
it all ends up covered
with slobber and hair.

Arthur the Artist

I'm Arthur. I'm an artist,
and I love to paint and draw.
I paint portraits on my forehead.
I draw landscapes on my jaw.

There's nothing quite as fun
as making sketches on my skin,
so I color on my elbows
and I scribble on my chin.

I'm known for doing doodles
on my fingers and my toes,
and my belly and my back are brushed
with beautiful tableaus.

I hope you'll come and see me
to appreciate my scrawls.
I am always in museums
where I hang upon the walls.

Just find the guy with ink and paint
on every body part.
Or, instead, just ask for me by name;
my friends all call me "Art."

im rlly gd @ txting

im rlly gd @ txting.
i do it all day lng.
im spedy on the keybrd
n my thms r supr strng.

i txt wth all my fmly.
i txt wth all my frnz.
n i rply 2 evry txt
tht nebdy senz.

id rthr keep on txting
thn go outsd n play.
i thnk i prbly snd abot
a thsnd txts a day.

im gld 2 no tht u cn
undrstnd me rlly wel.
4 if u cldnt rd my txts
id haf to lrn to spel.

Learning to Fly

I'm soaring.
I'm sailing.
I'm learning to fly.
I'm leaping.
I'm bouncing.
I'm high in the sky.

I'm jumping.
I'm hopping.
I'm up in the air.
I'm dashing.
I'm diving,
the wind in my hair.

I'm swooping.
I'm whooshing.
I'm light as a kite.
I'm flittering,
fluttering,
floating in flight.

I'm toppling.
I'm tumbling.
I'm falling. I crashed.
And, whoopsie,
my parents
new mattress is trashed.

My Sister's Pretty Picky

My sister's pretty picky.
She likes to pick a fight.
She always wants to pick the film
on family movie night.

She picks her teeth with toothpicks.
She's skilled at picking locks.
She picks her Minecraft pickaxe
to pick away at blocks.

She's always picking flowers.
She picks on her guitar.
She's even picky when she's
picking out a candy bar.

I only wish that, now and then,
she might pick up her clothes.
I also wish she wasn't
quite so picky with her nose.

Cats in the Kitchen

Cats in the kitchen asleep in the sink.
Cats in the litter box making a stink.
Cats in the living room clawing the couch.
Cats in the closet at play in a pouch.

Cats in the bedroom destroying the bedding.
Cats on the table tops rolling and shedding.
Cats in the bathroom inspecting the tub.
Out in the flowerbed under a shrub.
Up on the windowsill grooming their fur.
Stretching and yawning, preparing to purr.
Waiting for someone to open a door.
Climbing a curtain. Exploring a drawer.
Maybe I'm crazy. You may say I'm bats.
Still, you can never have too many cats.

I'm a Pirate Ballerina

I'm a pirate ballerina
on a pirate sailing ship.
In my purple pirate leotard
I like to spin and skip.

I prance around the poop deck
leaping lightly on my toes
in my purple pirate tutu
and my bustle and my bows.

I wiggle on the rigging
and I dance around the mast,
shouting, "Yo, ho, ho, me hearties!"
and, "Ahoy there!" or "Avast!"

I'm sure you'd think it's strange
to see me jump around and gyrate,
but this is rather normal
for a ballerina pirate.

If you wonder why I do this,
it's a fairly simple answer...
My mother was a pirate
and my father was a dancer.

Roses Are Red

Roses are red
(it has often been said),
and so is the welt
swelling up on my head.

Violets are blue
(I've no doubt that it's true).
The bruise that I've got
on my cheekbone is too.

Daisies are white
(I expect this is right),
and so is my face
as I've had quite a fright.

That's why this tip
isn't something to skip:
It's fine to give flowers,
but try not to trip.

It's Raining in My Bedroom

It's raining in my bedroom.
It's been this way all week.
I think the upstairs neighbor's plumbing
might have sprung a leak.

They may be on vacation.
They must be out of town.
And, all the while, my bedroom rain
continues pouring down.
My shoes have gotten soggy.
My bed is growing mold.
A pond is forming on my floor.
It's all so wet and cold,
that frogs have started spawning.
An otter wandered through
with salmon splashing upstream,
and some guy in a canoe.
Now waves are growing larger.
The weather's turning grim.
A tide is rising rapidly.
I'm glad that I can swim.
My parents called the plumber.
He's nowhere to be seen.
Does anybody know where I
can buy a submarine?

My Invisible Dragon

I have an invisible dragon.
She's such a remarkable flyer.
She soars through the sky on invisible wings
exhaling invisible fire.

My dragon is utterly silent.
She soundlessly swoops through the air.
Why, she could be flying beside you right now,
and you'd never know she was there.

And if you should reach out to pet her,
I don't think you'd notice too much.
Her body is simply too airy and light
to sense her by means of a touch.

And just as you don't see or hear her,
and just as she cannot be felt,
my dragon does not have an odor at all,
which means that she'll never be smelt.

Although you may find this outlandish,
you just have to trust me, it's true.
And, oh, by the way, did I mention I have
an invisible unicorn too?

If I Had a Dollar

If I had a dollar
I know what I'd do;
I'd go to the mall
and I'd spend it on you.

I'd shop for a shoelace,
or maybe a sock,
or maybe a ribbon,
or maybe a rock.

I'd pay for a pickle,
a pear, or a plum.
I'd get you a grape,
or a half-pack of gum.

I'd spring for some string
if the string were on sale.
I'd purchase a pinky-sized
pink plastic pail.

I'd pick up a pencil,
I'd give you a stick.
I'd buy you a bit of
a board or a brick.

I like you, I do,
but I'm sorry to say
you can't get a lot
for a dollar today.

I Lost My Head

Before I go to sleep each night
I first remove my head,
and set it gently down upon
the nightstand by my bed.
And every morning when I wake,
I stretch my arms and yawn,
then pick my head up carefully
and put it right back on.

I put my head on backward
when I woke up yesterday,
and, every time I turned my head,
I looked the other way.
I started walking into walls
and falling down the stairs.
I stumbled into tables
and I tumbled over chairs.

Today is looking even worse;
I woke up in my bed
and felt around my nightstand
but I couldn't find my head.
I hope I find it shortly.
I'd be sad if it were gone.
From now on when I go to bed
I think I'll leave it on.

No Pencil

No pencil.
No marker.
No paint brush.
No pen.
No nothing
to draw with
or paint with
again.

No blue paint.
No green paint.
No pink paint.
No red.
Mom takes them
away when
I color
my head.

Catastrophe

Our house is a catastrophe.
The curtains are in shreds.
There's fur on all the furniture
and "presents" on our beds.

The couch is clawed to pieces.
The bathroom rug is ripped.
The goldfish bowl is broken
and the cat food dish is flipped.

There's kitty litter everywhere.
The carpet smells like pee.
We went away for just one day
and got CATastrophe.

The Technobabylonians

The Technobabylonians,
they babble night and day.
They talk about computers,
though they've nothing much to say.

They gab about their gadgets
and the tech that's in their toys.
I hear the words they're speaking
but it simply sounds like noise.

They yak about their tablets
and they crow about their phones.
They talk about technology
that no one even owns.

They use the latest jargon
as they jabber on and on.
I'm baffled by their yammering.
It makes me want to yawn.

I'm sure they're saying something
as they gabble on with glee,
but I can't understand a word.
It's all just Geek to me.

Elementary

"Elementary."
That means "easy."
I don't find it
quite so breezy.

Learn addition.
Then subtraction.
Multiply.
Divide a fraction.
Spelling. Science.
Reading. Writing.
Social studies.
Speech reciting.
Testing. Testing.
Still more Testing.
Not much recess.
Not much resting.

I complained but
no one listened.
Maybe elementary
isn't.

I Bought a Balloon

I bought a balloon that weighs more than a pound.
I can't make it float. It just drags on the ground.
I drag it behind me wherever I go.
It wasn't the smartest decision. I know.
So that's why I'm thinking, the next time around,
I'll only buy one that weighs *less* than a pound.

Mr. Yes and Mr. No

Mr. Yes and Mr. No
could not decide which way to go.

They walked all day. They walked all night.
They first turned left, and then turned right.
They ran along a railroad track
then turned around and came right back.
They wandered in and out of town.
They hiked up hills and stumbled down.
They strolled in straight lines, circles, squares.
They climbed up ladders, stomped down stairs,
but everywhere they ever went
they wound up there by accident
because the two could not agree
on where to go or what to see.

We don't know where they are today.
They've wandered off and gone astray.
And no one has the slightest guess
where Mr. No and Mr. Yes
have ended up and might be found;
perhaps upstairs or underground,
or in a cab, or overseas,
or on the shores of Lake Louise,
or paddling up the Amazon.
That is to say, they're simply gone.

But if they do turn up one day
I think it might be best if they
decided not to rove and roam,
like Mr. Maybe.
He's at home.

Our Mother Threw the Pie Away

Our mother threw the pie away.
She dumped out all the Cokes.
She kept the beans and leafy greens
and leeks and artichokes.

She chucked the cheese and chocolate chips.
She pitched the pudding out,
but kept the beets and broccoli
and jars of sauerkraut.

She canned the cakes and cookies
and she ditched the doughnuts too,
but kept the kale and carrot sticks
and celery and tofu.

She jettisoned the junk food.
She tossed out every treat.
So now our house has only foods
that no one wants to eat.

This happens to us every year.
It seems to be our fate.
Our mom goes on a diet
and we *all* start losing weight.

Oh My Darling, Frankenstein

(sing to the tune of "Clementine")

Oh my darling,
oh my darling,
oh my darling,
Frankenstein.
I abhor you
and adore you.
You're my darling,
Frankenstein.

Your creator
was a doctor
in a castle
near the Rhine.
On a slab
inside his lab
you were constructed,
Frankenstein.

Arms and legs and
head and torso,
that the doctor
did combine.
Bolts of lighting,
very frightening,
gave you life, dear
Frankenstein.

Then you rose up
from the table
with a bellow
and a whine.
You went lurching,
simply searching
for some dinner,
Frankenstein.

When the townsfolk
saw you coming,
you sent shivers
down their spines.
So they chased you
with their pitchforks
and their torches,
Frankenstein.

Then you lumbered
to the forest,
where you hid
amongst the pine
while the doc, he
did concoct me—
yes, a bride
for Frankenstein.

We were married
in the castle,
and forever
you'll be mine.
We're a creature
double feature,
oh my darling,
Frankenstein.

A Pug Is a Dog

A pug is a dog
with a curlicue tail.
He eats like a hog
and he snores like a whale.
He's flat in the snout
and his belly is big.
The pug came about
just by misspelling pig.

I'm Learning to Play the Piano Today

I'm learning to play the piano today.
Tomorrow I'll learn the guitar.
The day after that I'll get good on the drums,
so I can become a big star.

The next day I'll learn how to sing and to rap,
and practice some dancing techniques.
And, that way, I'm sure to be famous and rich
in no more than one or two weeks.

I just told my mother my excellent plan,
explaining the millions I'll earn.
She told me that, firstly, I'll need to learn patience.
So, how long will that take to learn?

I Sort of Have the Sniffles

I sort of have the sniffles.
It seems as if I'll sneeze.
I'm slightly showing signs
of some disorder or disease.

It could be I'm contagious.
Perchance I have a chill.
It's feeling like a fever.
I've an inkling that I'm ill.

I might have mild myalgia.
I'm probably in pain.
It looks as if I'm lately
more susceptible to strain.

The likelihood it's lethal
is maybe minuscule.
But why take any chances?
I'll be staying home from school.

To Some It's Known as Halloween

To some it's known as "Halloween,"
or else "All Hallows Eve."
To some it's simply "Dress Up Day,"
a time for make-believe.

And some folks call it "Trick or Treat,"
when ghosts and witches play.
To others it's the night before
the day called "All Saints Day."

It's got so many different names,
but this is what I say:
To me October thirty-first
is called "Free Candy Day."

I Found Myself upon a Cow

It happened once, I don't know how,
I found myself upon a cow.
The cow was startled, too, to see
that she was sitting under me.
And underneath the cow, a hog
was resting right atop a dog.

Below them in this lofty heap
were piled a goat, a duck, a sheep,
a buffalo, a horse, a yak,
and at the bottom of the stack,
a rather worried-looking cat,
extremely wide and very flat.

So if you never want your cat
to wind up wide and round and flat
then learn this lesson here and now:
Don't ever sit upon a cow.

Modern Popularity

I have a half a million friends.
I'm popular. It's true!
I like them, each and every one,
and they all like me too.

I have more friends than anybody
else you've ever known.
It's nice to have so many friends.
I never feel alone.

They come from countries near and far,
from countries large and little.
Afghanistan and Zambia
and places in the middle.

From Austria to India,
from Norway to Nepal,
my friends are from so many countries
I can't count them all.

I hope someday I'll meet my friends.
You see, we've never met.
The only way I know them all
is on the Internet.

My Brother's a Genius

My brother's a genius;
as smart as they come.
Without his computer, though,
boy, is he dumb.
His screws all get looser.
His lights become dim.
His mind starts unwinding.
His senses grow slim.

His IQ starts dropping.
His smarts start to sink.
It seems to be strenuous
even to think.
His wisdom and wits take
a little vacation.
His head is still there
but his brain leaves the station.

He can't answer questions
or speak off the cuff.
His noggin gets clogged up
with feathers and fluff.
He's dense as a doorknob.
He's thick as a brick.
It's plain that his brain
can't compete with a stick.

When using computers,
he's bright as the sun.
Without them, he's dumb
as a hamburger bun.
He's slow as a dodo,
obtuse as a trout.
I sure hope our Internet
never goes out.

Brody the Emoticon

Brody the emoticon
is famous for his style,
and if you ever meet him,
you will likely see his :-)

But if you come across him
on a day he's feeling down,
instead of giving you a :-)
he'll look at you and :-(

On other days he'll ;-) at you.
He'll sometimes blow a :-*
and if he's feeling playful
he'll stick out his :-P like this.

But, oftentimes, he's simply bored
and can't resist a :-O
because there's nothing else to do
for an emoticon.

Dizzy Dottie's Dog Salon

At Dizzy Dottie's Dog Salon
we'll fix your fido's fur.
We will clip and comb his canine coat
and color his coiffure.

We will primp your pomeranian
and gussy up your pug.
We will brush your beagle's back
and scrub his scruffy little mug.

Could your poodle use a crew-cut?
Does your boxer need a bob?
Want an afro for your spaniel?
Come let Dottie's do the job.

Get your setter new extensions.
Send your shepherd for a shave.
Bring your harrier for highlights
or your whippet for a wave.

From a bouffant to a beehive,
from a buzz-cut to a bun,
all the hair-dos here at Dottie's
are affordable and fun.

Drive your doggy down to Dottie's
for our groomings and shampoos,
where we don't do cuts for kitties
but we do do doggy dos.

Sam, Who Only Ate Jam

There was a boy whose name was Sam.
The only thing he ate was jam.
When offered any other food,
he'd claim he wasn't in the mood.
He'd say, "I'm fairly full today,"
and push that other food away.

And so he never tasted pie,
or gave spaghetti sauce a try,
and even if you asked him, "Please?"
he wouldn't chew on cheddar cheese.
He couldn't stand potato chips.
Bananas never crossed his lips.
And not a bit of beef or lamb
or deviled egg or candied yam
would wind up on his dinner plate,
for jam was all he ever ate.

Now, as it happened, late one day
poor Sam expired. He passed away.
We don't know why. It might have been
some mineral or vitamin
was missing from the food he ate
and caused this clearly awful fate,
or maybe all that sugar made
him fall to pieces, start to fade,
until the day that eating jam
at last became the end of Sam.

We can't be certain why he died
but, maybe, if he'd only tried
some yogurt or some celery,
a piece of toast, a pear, a pea,
a pizza crust, a grain of rice,
a half an herb, a single spice,
a spoon of soup with just one clam,
then, maybe, we would still have Sam.

Alas, he never ate a grape
or chocolate bar or Belgian crepe
or lobster bisque or Irish stew
or sauerkraut or cheese fondue
or casserole or sloppy joe,
so this is all we'll ever know:
Since jam was all he had to eat,
his life was rather short and sweet.

I Sat Down on a Seesaw

I sat down on a seesaw
to see what I could see,
but all I saw was seesaw
rising up in front of me.

I couldn't see the treetops.
I couldn't see the sky.
I couldn't see the far-off fields.
I sat and wondered why.

I couldn't see the swing set,
or even see the slide.
I guess I need someone to
sit down on the other side.

Lorenzo Liszt, Non-Scientist

Lorenzo Liszt, non-scientist,
researches things that don't exist.
He looks for fur from fish and frogs
and scales that came from cats and dogs.

He hunts for things like hamster wings
and walruses with wedding rings.
He analyzes famous flies
and speculates on oysters' eyes.

He contemplates the common traits
of rattlesnakes on roller skates,
and then explores for dinosaurs
who shop in corner grocery stores.

He thinks about the desert trout.
He studies underwater drought.
He ponders how the purple cow
remained unnoticed up till now.

He scans the skies for flying pies
and tests for turtles wearing ties
and bears who buzz and beep because...
well, this is what Lorenzo does.

Although we feel that he should deal
with something that's a bit more real,
Lorenzo Liszt just can't resist
researching things that don't exist.

I Think, *ACHOO!*, I Have the Flu

I think, *ACHOO!*, I have the flu.
I'm sneezing, and *ACHOO! ACHOO!*
I'm not sure what, *ACHOO!*, to do.
You say, *ACHOO!*, don't sneeze on you?
ACHOO! Whoops. Now you've got it too.

Gobble, Gobble Went the Turkey

"Gobble, gobble," went the turkey
in his quirky chirping way.
"Gobble, gobble," went the turkey
up until Thanksgiving Day.

"Gobble, gobble," went the turkey
till we turned the oven on.
Gobble, gobble went the turkey.
Now the turkey's (gobble) gone.

Mr. Mirror

The man called Mr. Mirror
is a most peculiar guy.
He looks a bit like everyone,
though no one quite knows why.

Mr. Mirror looks like you.
He also looks like me.
When anybody looks at him,
it's just themselves they see.

The President will tell you
Mr. Mirror looks like him.
My Uncle Jim is certain
he resembles Uncle Jim.

To people with a mustache
Mr. Mirror has one too.
He looks like people wearing hats
and those who never do.

He looks like someone five years old,
and someone ninety nine.
He looks like someone with a cold,
and someone feeling fine.

He looks like someone very short
and someone super tall.
but Mr. Mirror doesn't look
like Dracula at all.

The Llama and the Aardvark

The llama loved the aardvark.
They were married in the spring.
They had a dozen babies
and their babies loved to sing.

So people came from miles around,
and this is what they saw:
twelve little baby llaardvarks
singing, "llaa llaa llaa llaa llaa."

A Pair of Potatoes Were Talking

A pair of potatoes were talking,
discussing what might be for lunch.
One turned to the other and told him,
"I think that I might have a hunch.
As long as we stay near the kitchen
and don't wander too far afield,
I'm sure that we'll see what they're serving.
We just have to keep our eyes peeled."

How Not to Make a Cardboard Fort

I found an empty cardboard box.
I made myself a fort.
I had to squeeze and twist and turn
and crumple and contort
to climb inside, but now I'm quite
embarrassed to report
I'm stuck inside this cardboard box
that's clearly much too short.
Has anybody got a box
that's bigger than a quart?

What a Ham!

My brother's always such a ham.
That's my biggest beef.
His puns are all so cheesy
and he will not lettuce leaf.

His gags are somewhat onionique.
They make us want to cry.
They're often sort of corny,
and they're never all that rye.

And even if we're chili,
in thyme he'll find a reason
to pepper us with salty jokes
no matter what the season.

I mustard up the courage
to dessert one afternoon.
He lightly toasted me and said,
"I'll ketchup with you soon."

But now I'm in a pickle.
See, a nickel's all I've got.
He says his jokes are ten cents each.
I mayo him a lot.

Jake the Yo-Yo Maker

I'm Jake, the yo-yo maker.
Making yo-yos is my thing.
It only takes a chunk of wood
and several feet of string.

To try to make sure every
single yo-yo is unique,
I make some from mahogany,
and turn some out in teak.

I fashion some from plastic,
and I build some out of brass.
I sculpt some out of stone,
or manufacture them from glass.

A scrap of patchy fabric here.
A shred of metal there.
I even made a yo-yo, once,
from Batman underwear.

Then, when I'm done constructing them,
I sell them on the street.
I'd say that making yo-yos
is a job that can't be beat.

It brings such joy and happiness;
I don't see many frowns.
But, just like any other job,
it has its ups and downs.

My Brother Is Still in His Bedroom

"My brother is still in his bedroom.
No doubt he'll be getting up soon.
But last night he stayed up till midnight,
so maybe he'll sleep until noon.

"I haven't gone into his bedroom.
Whenever I do he gets mad.
If anyone woke him this morning,
I'm guessing it must have been dad.

"It's probably best not to bug him.
I try to stay out of his way."
Yes, that's what I said when mom asked me
if I woke up grumpy today.

Too Many Chickens

My chickens all had chicks
and I've got more than I can keep.
Perhaps you'd like to purchase one?
They're cheap, cheap, cheep!

I'm Told By My Snail

I'm told by my snail that he will not get dressed.
He says that he's not feeling well.
It's not that he won't wear a coat or a vest;
he won't even put on his shell.

He's still in his bed as he lets out a yawn.
I tell him I think it's okay
to wait till tomorrow to put his shell on
since he's feeling sluggish today.

Today Is the Day

I'm happy to say that today is the day.
I'm super excited. I'm shouting, "Hooray!"

I woke up delighted and ready to go.
My mind is abuzz and my eyes are aglow.

There's no doubt about it. It's perfectly clear.
The time is upon us. The moment is here.

I'm eager and keen for the action to start,
and when it begins I'll be playing my part.

I'll jump in the bustle and I'll give it my all.
I'm certain that soon I'll be having a ball.

But where should I go now, and what should I do?
I'm hoping that someone will give me a clue.

I'm not sure what's happening. All I can say
is yesterday's gone, so today is the day.

Index

ABOUT THE AUTHOR

Children's Poet Laureate Kenn Nesbitt is the author of many books for children, including *The Armpit of Doom*, *More Bears!*, *The Tighty-Whitey Spider*, and *My Hippo Has the Hiccups*. He is also the creator of the world's most popular children's poetry website, www.poetry4kids.com.

More Books by Kenn Nesbitt

Kiss, Kiss Good Night – Snuggle up with this bedtime poem, all about how mommy animals say good night to their little ones. Cartwheel Books. ISBN: 978-0545479578.

The Armpit of Doom – Seventy new poems about crazy characters, funny families, peculiar pets, comical creatures, and much, much more. ISBN: 978-1477590287.

I'm Growing a Truck in the Garden – Follow one boy through his day as he plays with his friends and creates havoc along the way. Collins Educational. ISBN: 978-0007462001.

The Ultimate Top Secret Guide to Taking Over the World – Are you fed up with people telling you what to do? You're in luck. All you have to do is read this book and carefully follow the instructions, and in no time at all you will be laughing maniacally as the world cowers before you. Sourcebooks Jabberwocky. ISBN: 978-1402238345.

MORE BEARS! – Kenn Nesbitt's picture book debut will have you laughing while shouting "More Bears!" along with the story's disruptive audience. The author/narrator keeps adding more and more bears, which he describes in humorous detail, until he gets fed up! The bears ride, dance, surf, and even somersault off the page. Sourcebooks Jabberwocky. ISBN: 978-1402238352.

The Tighty-Whitey Spider: And More Wacky Animals Poems I Totally Made Up – Following up the bestselling collection, *My Hippo Has the Hiccups*, Kenn Nesbitt dares to go where no poet has gone before. With poems like and "I Bought Our Cat a Jetpack" and "My Dog Plays Invisible Frisbee," this collection shines bright with rhymes that are full of jokes, thrills, and surprises. Sourcebooks Jabberwocky. ISBN: 978-1402238338.

My Hippo Has the Hiccups: And Other Poems I Totally Made Up - *My Hippo Has the Hiccups* contains over one hundred of Kenn's newest and best-loved poems. The dynamic CD brings the poems to life with Kenn reading his own poetry, cracking a joke or two, and even telling stories about how the poems came to be. Sourcebooks Jabberwocky. ISBN: 978-1402218095.

Revenge of the Lunch Ladies: The Hilarious Book of School Poetry – From principals skipping school to lunch ladies getting back at kids who complain about cafeteria food, school has never been so funny. Meadowbrook Press. ISBN: 978-1416943648.

When the Teacher Isn't Looking: And Other Funny School Poems – *When the Teacher Isn't Looking* may be the funniest collection of poems about school ever written. This collection of poems by Kenn Nesbitt is sure to have you in stitches from start to finish. Meadowbrook Press. ISBN: 978-0684031286.

The Aliens Have Landed at Our School – No matter what planet you live on, this book is packed with far-out, funny, clever poems guaranteed to give you a galactic case of the giggles. Meadowbrook Press. ISBN: 978-0689048647.

For more funny poems, visit
www.poetry4kids.com

Made in the USA
San Bernardino, CA
07 October 2014